Amazing

Asparagus

Learn to Cook Asparagus in a Variety of Ways!

BY: Nancy Silverman

COPYRIGHT NOTICES

My Heartfelt Thanks and A Special Reward for Your Purchase!

https://nancy.gr8.com

My heartfelt thanks at purchasing my book and I hope you enjoy it! As a special bonus, you will now be eligible to receive books absolutely free on a weekly basis! Get started by entering your email address in the box above to subscribe. A notification will be emailed to you of my free promotions, no purchase necessary! With little effort, you will be eligible for free and discounted books daily. In addition to this amazing gift, a reminder will be sent 1-2 days before the offer expires to remind you not to miss out. Enter now to start enjoying this special offer!

Table of Contents

(1) Stuffed Fish with Asparagus

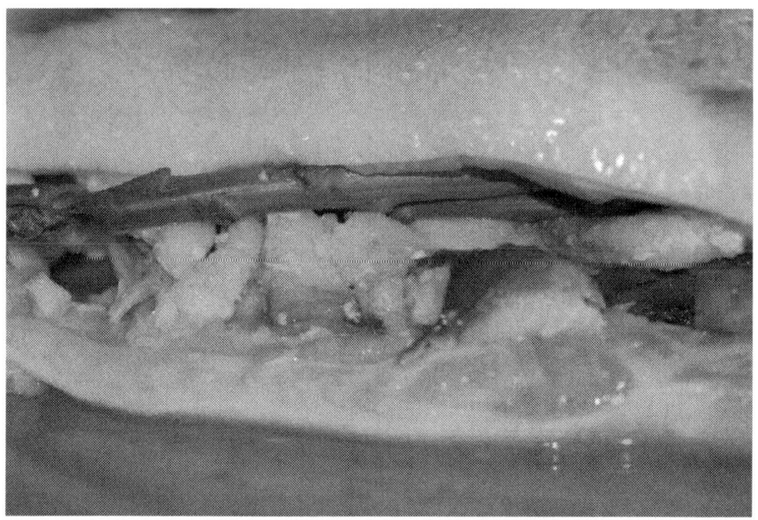

Cod, flounder or snapper are all great fish to use to make this recipe. Make sure you do purchase some fresh asparagus and use the best cheese for this recipe (I think the best is a mixture). Even your picky eaters might dare taste this very fancy and tender baked fish.

Yield: 4

Total Prep Time: 45 minutes

Ingredient List:

- 4 Cod filets
- ¼ pound fresh trimmed asparagus
- 2 cups baby spinach
- 1 package cream cheese, room temperature
- Salt, pepper
- 2 minced cloves garlic
- 2 tablespoons chopped fresh chives
- 1 Tablespoon red pepper flakes
- 1 teaspoon onion powder
- 1 cup seasoned panko crumbs
- ½ cup shredded Parmesan cheese
- 2 tablespoons unsalted butter
- 1 large egg

Instructions:

1. Preheat oven to 400 degrees F.
2. Grease a large baking dish and set aside.
3. Place the fish filets on a flat surface and season with salt and pepper. Try to choose flat large filets, as it will be easier to stuff them.
4. Now prepare thc stuffing. Heat the butter and cook the garlic, chives, and spinach for 5 minutes.
5. In a saucepan, heat water with salt and steam the asparagus.
6. Cook the asparagus for about 12 minutes and then cut into small pieces.
7. Place the cooked veggies in a mixing bowl and add the cream cheese, salt, pepper, onion powder, and red pepper flakes and combine well.
8. In a second bowl, whisk the egg.
9. In a third bowl, mix the Parmesan cheese and the crumbs.
10. Proceed to dip each fish filet in the egg and then the breading.
11. Lay the fish filets on the baking dish, apply a generous portion of the stuffing on the fish and then roll each filet tightly.
12. Use toothpicks to hold fish together.
13. Bake in the oven for 30 minutes.

(2) Asparagus Soufflé

A soufflé is made with some eggs, egg whites to be more specific, and some other awesome ingredients, such as cheese. Asparagus soufflé is no different and you will absolutely love discovering this recipe that will leave no one indifferent.

Yield: 4

Total Prep Time: 40 minutes

Ingredient List:

- 1-pound fresh trimmed asparagus
- 6 egg whites
- Salt, pepper
- ½ dried mustard
- 1 cup soy milk
- ½ cup all-purpose flour
- 2 minced cloves garlic
- ¼ cup mixed parsley, thyme, and basil
- 2 tablespoons unsalted butter
- 1/2 cup grated Gruyere cheese

Instructions:

1. Preheat the oven to 400 degrees F.
2. Blanch the asparagus by cooking them in boiling water for 4 or 5 minutes, then set aside.
3. Then when they have cooled, puree them in the blender with the garlic, mixed herbs, dried mustard, and salt and pepper. Save that mixture.
4. Next, make the sauce. Boil the milk, then add the all-purpose flour and the butter.
5. Reduce the heat to low, stirring constantly until no more lumps are showing. Add the cheese and continue stirring until all is well blended.
6. Now, mix the sauce with the asparagus mixture in a large bowl and whisk in the egg whites.
7. Pour this mixture into individual ramekins or a larger one.
8. Bake in the oven for 40 minutes, until the surface is golden.

(3) Ground turkey and asparagus delight

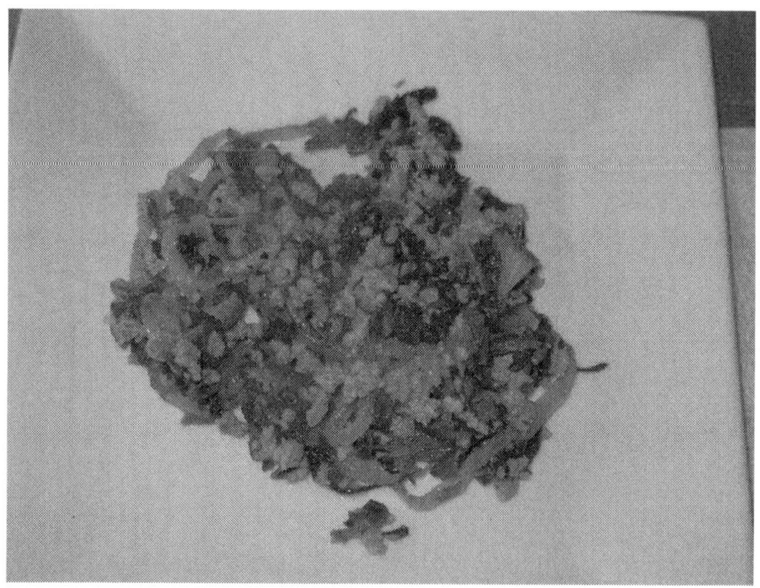

What a fun way and different way to serve asparagus and ground meat. I have to say I prefer using ground chicken or ground turkey for this recipe to keep it low fat, but if you eat beef, go ahead and use ground beef, it is okay.

Yield: 4

Total Prep Time: 30 minutes

Ingredient List:

- 1-pound ground turkey or ground chicken
- 3 minced cloves garlic
- ½ chopped yellow onion
- 6-8 trimmed fresh asparagus
- 1 cup cooked brown rice
- Salt, pepper
- 1 teaspoon dried cumin
- 1 Tablespoon olive oil

Instructions:

1. In a large skillet, cook the ground meat with a little oil and the garlic and onion.
2. Meanwhile, use the steamer basket and a saucepan to boil water and steam the asparagus for about 5 or 6 minutes. Let them cool down and cut them in halves or thirds.
3. Once the meat is cooked, drain the excess fat very well and place back in the skillet.
4. Leave the heat on low and add the cooked rice, the asparagus, salt, pepper and cumin.
5. Stir very well to combine.
6. Your ground meat and asparagus dish is ready. You could use tortillas to make some burritos with it or just eat it as is maybe even with a side of sour cream.

(4) Salmon and Asparagus with Lemon Sauce

Don't underestimate the taste of asparagus cooked with salmon fillets. Use the right toppings and cook the salmon on a bed of asparagus. This is a fantastic dish, both in flavor and appearance.

Yield: 4

Total Prep Time: 45 minutes

Ingredient List:

- 4 salmon filets
- 2 tablespoons lemon and pepper seasoning
- 2 tablespoons lemon juice
- 1 teaspoon lemon zest
- ½ pound fresh asparagus
- 3 minced cloves garlic
- ¼ cup shredded Parmesan cheese
- Olive oil
- Salt, pepper

IIIIIIIIIIIIIIIIIIIIIIIIIIIIIIIIIIIIIIIIIIIIIIIIIIIIIIIIIIIIII

Instructions:

1. Preheat the oven to 400 degrees F.
2. Prepare a baking dish by greasing it and set it aside.
3. Use fresh asparagus that you have trimmed.
4. Lay them in the baking dish, season it with salt pepper, garlic, lemon juice and lemon zest.
5. Lay the salmon on top and season with the lemon and pepper seasonings, then sprinkle the Parmesan cheese on top.
6. Bake this fabulous dish in the oven for 30 minutes or so.

(5) Asparagus flatbread awesome idea

You can use flatbread, because we can guarantee it is tasty and we love it. You could also use French bread to make this recipe, and it would be just as good, and don't spare the garlic!

Yield: 2

Total Prep Time: 45 minutes

Ingredient List:

- 2 medium flatbreads
- 8 trimmed fresh asparagus
- ¼ cup chopped red onion
- Salt, pepper
- 1 Tablespoon fresh chopped parsley
- 1 Tablespoon fresh chopped thyme
- ½ cup Alfredo sauce
- 1 cup shredded Swiss cheese

IIIIIIIIIIIIIIIIIIIIIIIIIIIIIIIIIIIIIIIIIIIIIIIIIIIIIIIIIII

Instructions:

1. Preheat the oven to 400 degrees F.
2. On a greased baking dish with a little olive oil, salt and pepper, cook the asparagus and red onions in the oven for about 12 minutes.
3. Meanwhile, get the other ingredients ready.
4. When the veggies are cooked, get them out, but leave the oven on.
5. Spread the Alfredo sauce on each flatbread, add the veggies, the fresh chopped herbs, and on top the shredded Swiss cheese.
6. Place back in the oven for another 25 minutes or until the cheese is completely melted.
7. This will be an awesome pizza.

(6) Spectacular Asparagus Burger Sandwich

If you want to make a special burger, use some fresh ground beef or even better ground lamb if you can. Then, prepare the asparagus and top the burger off with it. This will certainly be a very unique burger, and you might be asked for the recipe more than once.

Yield: 4

Total Prep Time: 40 minutes

Ingredient List:

- 1-pound ground fresh lamb
- 1 Tablespoon chopped fresh mint
- 2 minced cloves garlic
- 1 egg yolk
- 8 fresh trimmed asparagus
- 1 Tablespoon Worcestershire sauce
- 1 Tablespoon lemon juice
- 1 Tablespoon olive oil
- Salt, pepper
- 4 Burger buns or Kaiser breads

IIIIIIIIIIIIIIIIIIIIIIIIIIIIIIIIIIIIIIIIIIIIIIIIIIIIIIIIIIIIIIIII

Instructions:

1. Making lamb burgers is pretty awesome on its own.
2. In a bowl, mix the lamb ground meat and add the fresh mint, garlic, lemon juice, Worcestershire sauce, salt, pepper, and egg yolk.
3. Use your hands to form 4 patties. Cook in olive oil until well done.
4. Meanwhile, steam the asparagus and get ready to assemble when done.
5. Use the burger buns, lamb patties, spicy mayonnaise and asparagus, yummy!

(7) Tofu, Asparagus and More

Tofu is a great way to get some protein without having to cook meat. Many vegetarians have adopted that food item in their regular meals, but if you just want a break from a heavy meal sometimes, this is a great option. However, remember that tofu is very plain so you have to serve it with a sauce or other tangy ingredients.

Yield: 4

Total Prep Time: 30 minutes

Ingredient List:

- Sesame oil
- 3 tablespoons sesame seeds
- 1 package firm tofu, cut in strips
- 2 tablespoons soy sauce
- 1 Tablespoon honey
- 1 Tablespoon red pepper flakes
- ½ cup vegetables broth
- 2 cups trimmed cut asparagus
- 1 chopped medium carrot
- 1 chopped yellow bell pepper
- 2 minced green onions
- 2 minced cloves garlic

IIIIIIIIIIIIIIIIIIIIIIIIIIIIIIIIIIIIIIIIIIIIIIIIIIIIIIIIIIIII

Instructions:

1. Make the sauce first. In a medium mixing bowl, combine the soy sauce, honey, sesame oil, red pepper flakes, and vegetable broth.
2. Use additional sesame oil to start cooking the sesame seeds, garlic, and onion in a skillet.
3. Add the tofu strips and the sauce and continue cooking.
4. Soon after, add the carrots, cut asparagus, and yellow bell pepper, and continue cooking until the asparagus are a little tender and the tofu browned.
5. Serve this great stir fry dish on a bed of egg noodles and enjoy fully without the heaviness of meat.

(8) Bacon Wrapped Asparagus

Bacon is good with almost anything, that's a fact. Asparagus is good with bacon, that's another fact. So let's proceed without any further discussion and make this mouthwatering appetizer for everyone.

Yield: 4

Total Prep Time: 40 minutes

Ingredient List:

- 1-pound fresh asparagus
- ½ pound turkey bacon
- 1/3 cup maple syrup
- 1 Tablespoon red pepper flakes

IIIIIIIIIIIIIIIIIIIIIIIIIIIIIIIIIIIIIIIIIIIIIIIIIIIIIIIIIIII

Instructions:

1. This dish is very easy to make and eat!
2. Preheat the oven at 425 degrees F.
3. On a baking sheet, wrap each asparagus with a slice of turkey bacon.
4. Mix the maple syrup with the red pepper flakes in small bowl and then brush on all the bacon wrapped asparagus before putting in the oven for 30-40 minutes.
5. Enjoy any day

(9) Asparagus Lasagna

I have to say when my husband said he had tasted a lasagna made with asparagus, I was a little skeptical. I had heard of spinach, eggplant, zucchinis, but asparagus- that was a first for me. So I made some trials and errors until I came up with this recipe has actually now been approved by my family committee!

Yield: 4

Total Prep Time: 60 minutes

Ingredient List:

- 8 precooked lasagna noodles
- 2 cups sliced fresh mushrooms
- 2 cups fresh trimmed and chopped asparagus
- ½ chopped sweet onion
- 2 cups whole milk
- 1 cup sour cream
- 1 tablespoon cornstarch
- Pinch nutmeg
- 2 tablespoons unsalted butter
- Salt, pepper
- 1 cup shredded parmesan
- 1 cup shredded mozzarella
- ½ cup seasoned breadcrumbs

Instructions:

1. Preheat oven to 400 degrees F.
2. Grease a large baking dish and set aside.
3. There are a few different steps to follow.
4. First, let's make the sauce. In a large saucepan, heat the butter and add the milk and bring to boil. Add the cornstarch and rcducc the heat to low temperature but stir consistently until the mixture thickens.
5. Add the sour cream, the nutmeg, and salt and pepper to the sauce and combine well, then keep on low heat.
6. In a skillet, heat some butter to cook the garlic, onion, mushrooms, and asparagus cut into pieces, for just about 5-6 minutes.
7. Next, assemble. You might need more or fewer lasagna noodles; keep in mind you need to cover the bottom of the baking dish first with a layer of noodles.
8. Add a generous portion of the sauce and the veggies. Follow by another layer of noodles, sauce, and veggies, and top if off with the noodles again.
9. On top of the last layer add the mixture of Swiss cheese and Parmesan cheese.
10. Finally sprinkle the breadcrumbs and place the dish in the oven for 45 minutes.
11. Serve warm with a side salad.

(10) Eggs, Smoked Salmon, and Asparagus Tart

Smoked salmon and asparagus must have been best friends in a prior life, because if I have these ingredients in my refrigerator, they will somehow always end up in the same dish. I am a big fan of this one, as I am a big fan of phyllo dough as well.

Yield: 4

Total Prep Time: 40 minutes

Ingredient List:

- 4 sheets phyllo dough
- ¼ pound trimmed cut fresh asparagus
- ¼ pound smoked salmon (chopped)
- Salt, pepper
- ¼ cup chopped red onion
- 2 tablespoons chopped fresh chives
- ½ package cream cheese
- 1 cup shredded Mozzarella cheese

IIIIIIIIIIIIIIIIIIIIIIIIIIIIIIIIIIIIIIIIIIIIIIIIIIIIIIIIIIII

Instructions:

1. Lay the phyllo dough on a greased baking sheet and then preheat the oven to 400 degrees F.
2. Precook the asparagus for 5 minutes, using hot boiling water. Then trim them and cut them into pieces.
3. Spread the cream cheese on the dough, then add the red onions, asparagus and chopped smoked salmon. Season with salt and pepper.
4. Sprinkle the whole thing with mozzarella cheese and bake in the oven for 25 to 30 minutes.

(11) Special Asparagus Au Gratin

I am pretty sure you had some potatoes au gratin or scalloped potatoes before. You might not have made them from scratch, but they are often an option on the restaurant menus. Asparagus au gratin is not much different, and requires cream and cheese and the right seasonings. Let's start cooking now!

Yield: 4

Total Prep Time: 45 minutes

Ingredient List:

- 1 Tablespoon all-purpose flour
- Pinch nutmeg
- Salt, pepper
- 1 cup heavy cream
- 1 cup whole milk
- 2 tablespoons unsalted butter
- ½ pound fresh trimmed asparagus
- 1 minced clove garlic
- 1 cup chopped red bell pepper
- ½ cup panko breadcrumbs

IIIIIIIIIIIIIIIIIIIIIIIIIIIIIIIIIIIIIIIIIIIIIIIIIIIIIIIIIIII

Instructions:

Preheat the oven to 375 degrees F.

You can use 4 small ramequins or a large one, or baking dish to prepare this recipe, depending on how you plan to serve it and what you have available.

Start the asparagus steaming and let them cook for about 5 minutes.

Then, in a medium saucepan, heat the butter and add both the milk and cream. Stir to combine.

Add the all-purpose flour next and bring to a boil, continuing to stir constantly.

Reduce the heat to low temperature. Your sauce should have thickened quite a bit. Season the sauce with salt, pepper, and nutmeg and let it simmer for now.

In a small skillet you will sauté the red bell pepper with garlic for 5 minutes.

You will then place the precooked veggies, including the asparagus, in the bottom of the baking dishes, add a generous portions of the sauce and top off with the breadcrumbs.

Bake in the oven for 30 minutes.

Serve warm as an appetizer or side dish.

(12) Fried Asparagus with Dipping Sauce

Asparagus tempura it is! I am telling you, this might be the new French fry of the decade. You really have to try it to understand what I am talking about. It is so good, that you will have to watch how many you eat, but you are getting some vitamins and mineral anyway from the veggie, so all in all, it's good.

Yield: 4

Total Prep Time: 40 minutes

Ingredient List:

- 1-pound fresh trimmed asparagus
- 2 cups tapioca or rice flour
- 1 teaspoon chili powder
- ½ teaspoon garlic powder
- ½ teaspoon onion powder
- 2 medium eggs
- 3 tablespoons whole milk
- Coconut oil for frying

Dipping sauce

- ¼ cup mayonnaise
- ¼ cup sour cream
- 2 minced green onions
- 1 Tablespoon lemon juice
- Salt, pepper
- Cayenne pepper

Instructions:

1. If you are using a deep fryer, there is no need to precook the asparagus; otherwise, give them a quick steam.
2. Combine the flours and seasonings in a bowl. This will be the breading.
3. In a second bowl, mix the eggs with the milk.
4. Star dipping each asparagus in the egg mixture, then the breading.
5. Fry in coconut oil if you can, as it will give it a very extra special taste.
6. When serving, use the recipe for the dipping sauce by combining all the ingredients listed above.
7. You can use that dipping sauce with chicken fingers as well.

(13) Asparagus Potage

This soup is scrumptious and you will love making it anytime of the year. I remember my roommate used to buy these dry mixes of cream of asparagus and heat some water and pretend it was soup. It looks good, but it really never did it for me. I have to say I was probably a food snob early on.

Yield: 4

Total Prep Time: 35 minutes

Ingredient List:

- 4 cups low fat turkey broth
- 1 cup half and half cream
- 1 medium white potato
- 1 small chopped yellow onion
- 1-pound fresh trimmed asparagus
- 2 tablespoons unsalted butter
- Salt, pepper
- 1 teaspoon chili powder

IIIIIIIIIIIIIIIIIIIIIIIIIIIIIIIIIIIIIIIIIIIIIIIIIIIIIIIIIIIIIIIIIIIIII

Instructions:

1. In a medium saucepan, bowl the water and cook the potatoes, after peeling them. I like to cut the potatoes at least in 4 pieces to make it easier.
2. At the same time, you can use a steamer basket on top of the saucepan and cook the asparagus.
3. In a large saucepan, heat the butter and cook the onion for 5 minutes.
4. Add the turkey broth, the cooked vegetables, and all seasonings, but keep a few asparagus son the side to decorate the soup with.
5. Keep on medium heat for now and add the heavy cream.
6. Stir to combine very well.
7. Place the soup in your high speed blender and activate until the mixture is smooth.
8. Pour the mixture back in the saucepan and heat on low temperature until you are ready to serve. Taste and adjust the seasonings as needed.
9. Decorate with a few trimmed pieces of asparagus.

(14) Asparagus Pasta Special Dish

I love asparagus with a white sauce. You can use white sauce in pasta, on a pizza, on a flatbread, or even in a casserole. Add meat (ham, chicken, bacon or prosciutto), and you have complete and tasty dish!

Yield: 4

Total Prep Time: 55 minutes

Ingredient List:

- 1 box or package of uncooked shells pasta
- 2 cups trimmed asparagus
- 1 cup chopped prosciutto ham
- Salt, pepper
- 1 can cream of celery
- 2 cups whole milk
- 1 cup shredded Parmesan
- Smoked paprika

||||||||||||||||||||||||||||||||||||||||||||||||||||||||||||

Instructions:

1. Preheat the oven to 400 degrees F. Grease a large baking dish.
2. Cook the pasta as you normally would, or according to the package. Drain well and set aside.
3. Basically combine all the Ingredient List: cream of celery, milk, salt, pepper, smoked paprika, and prosciutto ham in the dish, add the cooked pasta and mix well.
4. Finally add the trimmed and cut asparagus and bake in the oven for about 45 to 50 minutes.

(15) Quinoa Salad with Beans and Asparagus

This is one powerful salad recipe. Quinoa is powerful, asparagus are super nutritious, and if you intend to add some black beans, you are in for a healthy treat. Don't underestimate the asparagus in these type of cold dishes, they taste great cold or warm.

Yield: 4

Total Prep Time: 40 minutes

Ingredient List:

- 2 cups tricolored uncooked quinoa
- 4 cups vegetable broth
- 1 bunch fresh asparagus trimmed
- 1 chopped medium zucchini
- 1/2 chopped red onion
- 1 can seasoned black beans, rinsed and drained
- 1 diced granny smith apple
- ¼ cup dried golden raisins
- Salt, pepper
- 2 tablespoons lemon juice
- 2 tablespoons white balsamic vinegar
- 2 tablespoons agave syrup
- 1 Tablespoon minced fresh ginger
- 1 Tablespoon minced cloves garlic
- ¼ cup olive oil
- 1 teaspoon turmeric powder

|||||||||||||||||||||||||||||||||||||||||||||||||||||||||||||||||||

Instructions:

1. First work on cooking the quinoa, by boiling the vegetables broth and follow the directions on the box or package.
2. Next, work on the dressing by combining the following Ingredient List: olive oil, lemon juice, garlic, turmeric powder, ginger, agave syrup, and balsamic vinegar. Set aside.
3. While the quinoa is cooking, steam the asparagus for about 6 or 7 minutes. Drain and cut in pieces after trimming them.
4. In a large mixing bowl, combine the cooked and cooled off quinoa, the precooked asparagus, the onion, the zucchinis, diced apples, black beans, and raisins.
5. Finally, pour the dressing you made earlier and mix with a wooden spoon to combine very well.
6. This salad can be served cold, it's a great one to bring on a picnic.

(16) Meatloaf with Asparagus

I have used asparagus in my burger patties and in my meatloaf quite often, too. I especially like the way it looks in the meatloaf when I slice it. It did take my kids a while to get used to it, I will be honest, but with time and patience, they all came around eventually.

Yield: 4

Total Prep Time: 40 minutes

Ingredient List:

- 1 cup fresh asparagus
- 1-pound lean ground beef
- 1 teaspoon dried mustard
- 2 tablespoons sweet chili sauce
- 2 tablespoons ketchup
- ½ medium sweet onion
- ½ cup panko breadcrumbs
- ½ cup rice flour
- 1 teaspoon garlic powder
- 1 large egg

||||||||||||||||||||||||||||||||||||||||||||||||||||||||||||||||||||

Instructions:

1. Preheat the oven to 375 degrees F.
2. Spray a loaf pan with non-stick oil.
3. Cook the asparagus first. If you want to take shortcut and cook them in the microwave, go for it.
4. Next, in a large mixing bowl, combine the ground meat, the dried mustard, sweet chili sauce, ketchup, sweet onion, garlic powder and cooked, chopped asparagus.
5. Add the egg, rice flour, and breadcrumbs.
6. Use your hands to mix well and press the mixture into the loaf pan.
7. Bake in the oven for 50 minutes.

(17) Asparagus Yummy Dip

Unusual does not mean uninteresting, actually it probably means quite the opposite. An asparagus dip is not something you encounter often, but now that I know how to make it, I wonder why. It has a lovely green color and very distinctive flavor to share with everyone.

Yield: 4

Total Prep Time: 20 minutes

Ingredient List:

- 1 ½ cups asparagus (fresh)
- 1 cup fresh chopped kale
- 2 minced cloves garlic
- ½ cup chicken broth
- 2 tablespoons sesame oil
- 2 tablespoons sesame seeds
- ½ tsp onion powder
- 1 teaspoon chili powder
- Salt, pepper

||||||||||||||||||||||||||||||||||||||||||||||||||||||||||||

Instructions:

1. This recipe is quite easy. Focus on cooking the asparagus first. I suggest to boil water and cook them with a little salt for 10-12 minutes. Drain and set aside.
2. Then simply add all the ingredients and the cooled off asparagus in the container of your high speed blender. Make sure to have removed any very hard ends of the asparagus they will not blend well.
3. Activate the blender until you reach a very smooth texture, a dip texture.
4. Taste and adjust the seasonings as needed.
5. Serve with raw veggies or crackers, or chips.

(18) Roasted Potatoes and Asparagus

I really enjoy mixing a few different types of potatoes when possible; yellow, white, purple, red… It is your choice, but it is prettier for sure. Mixing some asparagus with the potatoes, along with another few key ingredients, will create this very tasty side dish.

Yield: 4

Total Prep Time: 40 minutes

Ingredient List:

- 2 sweet potatoes
- 2 yellow potatoes
- 3 tablespoons avocado oil
- 2 minced cloves garlic
- 1 large diced avocado
- Salt, pepper
- ¼ pound fresh trimmed asparagus
- 1 Tablespoon lemon juice
- 1 Tablespoon Dijon mustard
- 1 Tablespoon balsamic vinegar

IIIIIIIIIIIIIIIIIIIIIIIIIIIIIIIIIIIIIIIIIIIIIIIIIIIIIIIIIIIIIIII

Instructions:

1. Start by peeling and dicing the potatoes. Then boil them for 10 minutes.
2. Also, trim the asparagus and cut it into small pieces.
3. Mix together in a small bowl the avocado oil, Dijon mustard, balsamic vinegar, lemon juice, salt, pepper.
4. Pour a bit of this dressing into a skillet, heat on medium heat and cook the asparagus pieces with the garlic.
5. Once the potatoes are cooked, add them to the asparagus and continue cooking all together.
6. When the veggies are cooked, add the diced avocado and serve as is with the leftover dressing.

(19) Warm Asparagus Salad

Let's keep it simple and healthy. Let's mix some cold and warm veggies together to prepare one of a kind salad. Also, let's mix together an awesome dressing that will bring this dish alive.

Yield: 4

Total Prep Time: 30 minutes

Ingredient List:

- 2 cups trimmed fresh asparagus
- 4 cups mixed greens
- 2 cups cherry tomatoes
- ½ chopped red onion
- 1 shredded medium carrot
- 1 cup crumbled blue cheese or goat cheese, your favorite
- 2 minced cloves garlic
- 3 tablespoons cup balsamic vinegar
- 1/2 cup olive oil
- 2 tablespoons coconut palm sugar
- Salt, pepper
- Smoked paprika

Instructions:

1. Preheat the oven to 400 degrees F.
2. On a greased baking sheet, place the trimmed asparagus, with the garlic, onion, and some olive oil. Season with salt and pepper.
3. Place in the oven for 15 minutes.
4. Meanwhile, prepare the other ingredients.
5. In a mixing bowl, prepare the dressing by combining the olive oil, the coconut palm sugar, balsamic vinegar, salt, pepper, and smoked paprika.
6. Start to assemble the salads, dividing the mixed greens on 4 plates.
7. Add all the other veggies on top, the cooked and raw ones (asparagus, onions tomatoes, carrots).
8. Drizzle the dressing on top and crumble blue cheese or goat cheese, your preference.

(20) Asparagus Delicious Cake

Now, this is an exceptional cake recipe, for sure. I really like to introduce this beautiful and special cake to my guests. They always are very surprised when they see a piece of asparagus on top of the cake… This kind of gives away the type of cake they are about to eat.

Yield: 6-8

Total Prep Time: 45 minutes

Ingredient List:

- ¼ pound trimmed fresh asparagus
- 2 cups cornmeal
- ½ cup brown sugar
- 3 large eggs
- 1 can coconut cream
- 2 tablespoons sour cream
- 1 teaspoon baking powder
- 1 teaspoon baking soda
- 1 teaspoon cinnamon

Instructions:

1. Preheat the oven to 350 degrees F. Grease a square dish and set it aside for now.
2. Use boiling water to steam the asparagus for about 15 minutes. You want them to be fully cooked.
3. In a mixing bowl mix the dry Ingredient List: corn meal, brown sugar, baking powder, baking soda, salt, and cinnamon.
4. In a different bowl, mix the eggs, sour cream, and coconut cream.
5. Then combine both mixtures, add the asparagus (chopped into tiny pieces) and mix well.
6. Pour the mixture into the baking dish and cook for about 40 minutes.
7. Remove and let it cool down before slicing and serving.

(21) Awesome Green Quiche

If you like quiche, and you are like me, I am pretty sure you don't mind what type of quiche you are served. I only dislike onion quiche, simply because it will be difficult for me to digest, any other type, bring it on. This asparagus quiche will make you wish you were born in France.

Yield: 4

Total Prep Time: 55 minutes

Ingredient List:

- Deep pie crust
- ½ pound chopped fresh asparagus
- ½ chopped sweet onion
- 2 minced cloves garlic
- 1 Tablespoon olive oil
- ¼ cup sliced black olives
- 1 cup diced fresh tomatoes
- ¼ cup fresh chopped herbs; mixed basil, oregano, parsley and thyme
- Salt, pepper
- Pinch cumin
- 2 cups cottage cheese
- 6 eggs
- 1 ½ cup shredded Parmesan cheese

IIIIIIIIIIIIIIIIIIIIIIIIIIIIIIIIIIIIIIIIIIIIIIIIIIIIIIIIIIIIIIIIIIIIII

Instructions:

1. Preheat the oven to 375 degrees F.
2. Boil water with salt and steam the asparagus for 10-12 minutes.
3. Meanwhile, in a skillet, heat and cook the garlic, onion, and all the fresh herbs.
4. In a large mixing bowl, whisk the eggs, and add the cottage cheese, salt, pepper, and cumin.
5. Add the cooked vegetables, the black olives, diced tomatoes, and combine well. Finally add the shredded Parmesan cheese.
6. Pour the eggs and veggie mixture into the pie crust.
7. Bake in the oven for 45 minutes.
8. Serve and enjoy warm.

(22) Sautéed Shrimp and Asparagus

Again, asparagus is such a vibrant green veggie, it goes perfectly with these pale pink shrimp. Don't forget to add some garlic and many types of seasonings. Make sure to also use some lemon zest and lemon juice.

Yield: 4

Total Prep Time: 40 minutes

Ingredient List:

- 1-pound medium shrimp, peeled and de-veined
- 1-pound fresh asparagus
- 3 minced cloves garlic
- 1 chopped yellow bell pepper
- ½ chopped red onions
- 3 tablespoons olive oil
- Salt, pepper
- 2 cups uncooked brown rice
- 4 cups vegetable broth

Instructions:

1. You still start a few things at once for this recipe. First, cook the rice as usual with the vegetable broth.
2. Then, start boiling water in saucepan and steaming the asparagus, after trimming them.
3. Next, in a large skillet, heat some olive oil and cook the garlic, red onion, and bell pepper.
4. Add the shrimp and stir. It should take about 10-12 minutes for the shrimp to be done or turn pink.
5. Once they are, add the cooked rice and the cooked cut asparagus and mix together.
6. Adjust the seasonings if needed, and serve with lemon wedges.

(23) Asparagus and Chicken Stir Fry

Asparagus is a great veggie to add to a stir fry, whether you are planning to use chicken or pork. What matters here is the sauce you will prepare to bring these ingredients together. And don't forget the rice! Stir fry should really be served on a bed of white or fried rice, your choice.

Yield: 4

Total Prep Time: 30 minutes

Ingredient List:

- 3 boneless and skinless chicken breasts
- ½ pound trimmed fresh asparagus
- 4 minced cloves garlic
- 2 minced green onions
- 1 chopped red bell pepper
- ½ cup vegetable broth
- 2 tablespoons teriyaki sauce
- 1 teaspoon orange zest
- ¼ cup orange juice
- 1 teaspoon cornstarch
- Salt, pepper
- Peanut oil
- Chopped peanuts

Instructions:

1. Prepare the chicken breasts; clean them, cut them in pieces and season them with salt and pepper.
2. In a large skillet, heat some peanut oil and start cooking the chicken, garlic and onions.
3. Steam the asparagus.
4. In a small saucepan, mix the following Ingredient List: orange juice, orange zest, peanut oil, teriyaki sauce, salt, pepper, and broth. Add the cornstarch and bring to boil, stirring constantly. Your sauce will be thicker and then reduce the temperature to low.
5. Add the bell peppers and the cooked asparagus to the chicken dish.
6. Once you know the chicken is cooked, pour the sauce on top and continue cooking all together for another 10 minutes or so.
7. I suggest serving with rice or rice noodles and sprinkled with chopped peanuts.

(24) Awesome Asparagus and Cheese Sandwiches

Surprise, surprise, let's use asparagus like we would for lettuce or arugula, or even spinach in our sandwich. Why not? Sure, it may take a few minutes more to prepare your sandwich, but it will be all worth it, I can promise you that much.

Yield: 4

Total Prep Time: 20 minutes

Ingredient List:

- Sandwich bread: ciabatta, focaccia, French bread or even Kaiser bread, your favorite will work
- 2 fresh asparagus per sandwich (8 in total)
- 1 cup Ricotta cheese
- 4 slices Swiss cheese
- Salt, pepper
- ½ teaspoon garlic powder
- ½ teaspoon onion powder

IIIIIIIIIIIIIIIIIIIIIIIIIIIIIIIIIIIIIIIIIIIIIIIIIIIIIIIIIIIIIIII

Instructions:

1. Preheat the oven to 400 degrees F.
2. First, steam the asparagus.
3. Meanwhile, mix together the ricotta cheese, garlic powder, salt, pepper and onion powder.
4. When the asparagus are cooked, place the sandwiches breads face open on a greased baking sheet.
5. Spread with the ricotta cheese mixture, and top with asparagus.
6. Add the Swiss cheese on top and place the sandwiches in the oven for about 10 minutes or until the cheese is melted.

(25) Asparagus Cakes

There is nothing better than asparagus cakes for lunch. This is truly a treat. When I make this recipe, there is never any leftovers (like I would hope for). I sometimes serve them on a bun, but honestly, most of the time, we simply eat them with our favorite dipping sauce.

Yield: 4

Total Prep Time: 20 minutes

Ingredient List:

- ½ pound fresh asparagus
- 1 cup sweet peas
- 1 cup sweet kernel corn
- 2 tablespoons flaxseeds
- 2 minced cloves garlic
- 1 rice flour
- ¼ cup cooked white basmati rice
- 2 tablespoons spicy salsa
- 1 large egg
- Salt, pepper
- Olive oil for cooking

Instructions:

1. -Cook the asparagus in boiling water- you want them to become soft but not mushy.
2. In a large mixing bowl, start mixing the following together: rice flour, rice, flaxseeds, garlic, corn, and peas. Add the egg and the seasonings and use your hands to mix all the ingredients together.
3. Once the asparagus stalks are cooked, chop them in small pieces and add them to the mixture with the salsa.
4. Mix again with your hands and start making the patties.
5. Heat some olive oil in a large skillet, and cook the cakes for 5 or 6 minutes on each side.
6. Let the excess oil absorb on paper toilet and serve with your favorite dipping sauce, perhaps even salsa.

About the Author

Nancy Silverman is an accomplished chef from Essex, Vermont. Armed with her degree in Nutrition and Food Sciences from the University of Vermont, Nancy has excelled at creating e-books that contain healthy and delicious meals that anyone can make and everyone can enjoy. She improved her cooking skills at the New England Culinary Institute in Montpelier Vermont and she has been working at perfecting her culinary style since graduation. She claims that her life's work is always a work in progress and she only hopes to be an inspiration to aspiring chefs everywhere.

Her greatest joy is cooking in her modern kitchen with her family and creating inspiring and delicious meals. She often says that she has perfected her signature dishes based on her family's critique of each and every one.

Nancy has her own catering company and has also been fortunate enough to be head chef at some of Vermont's most exclusive restaurants. When a friend suggested she share some of her outstanding signature dishes, she decided to add cookbook author to her repertoire of personal achievements. Being a technological savvy woman, she felt the e-book realm would be a better fit and soon she had her first cookbook available online. As of today, Nancy has sold over 1,000 e-books and has shared her culinary experiences and brilliant recipes with people from all over the world! She plans on expanding into self-help books and dietary cookbooks, so stayed tuned!

Author's Afterthoughts

Thank you for making the decision to invest in one of my cookbooks! I cherish all my readers and hope you find joy in preparing these meals as I have.

There are so many books available and I am truly grateful that you decided to buy this one and follow it from beginning to end.

I love hearing from my readers on what they thought of this book and any value they received from reading it. As a personal favor, I would appreciate any feedback you can give in the form of a review on Amazon and please be honest! This kind of support will help others make an informed choice on and will help me tremendously in producing the best quality books possible.

My most heartfelt thanks,

Nancy Silverman

If you're interested in more of my books, be sure to follow my author page on Amazon (can be found on the link Bellow) or scan the QR-Code.

https://www.amazon.com/author/nancy-silverman

Made in the USA
Columbia, SC
21 December 2022